SURROUNDING FACTORS

EXPLORE WHAT DETERMINES THE SUCCESS OF NBA GREATS

PROBY SHANDILYA

to Mr. Trevor Gamba,

Hope you enjoy the book!

Proby Shandilya

WWW.PROBYSPORTZ.COM

For any inquiries regarding this book, please email:
probyshan@gmail.com

ISBN: 978-1-7324110-1-2

First Edition May 2018

CONTENTS

To my little Sister, my Mom and Dad

ACKNOWLEDGMENTS

This book came out of my love for the game of basketball. I'm grateful to all that have instilled that love in me: my coaches, teammates, friends and family.

Thanks to Uncle Vis Valluri, who's been more a friend and given me constant encouragement since my elementary school days with basketball statistics and analysis.

A special and sincere thank you to Michelle Kandah for a wonderful job with proofreading, editing and her suggestions to make this book an easy read.

Thanks to coach Jeff Roper of Saratoga National Junior Basketball League for years of encouragement and for giving me an opportunity to lead a division 3 team as head coach.

To Joe Kaiser, who I look up to as a sports writer and a source of inspiration.

To NBA and NCAA players, coaches and management staff from whom I've learnt so much just by watching and reading about them.

I'm extremely grateful to my parents for their love,

constant support and encouragement throughout the process of bringing this idea to life in the form of this book. A shout-out to my little sister, who made me smile and kept me going when nights got long finishing up my research for this book.

INTRODUCTION

NBA commissioner, David Stern announced: "With the 11th pick in the 2006 NBA draft, the Orlando Magic select J.J. Redick from Duke University." Applause followed as J.J. Redick walked proudly onto the stage to be crowned the next shooting guard for the Orlando Magic. J.J. Redick, a storied college basketball player that was picked by one of the premier NBA franchises headed to Orlando with plenty of promise. But, in the years that followed, he fell way short of all expectations and was traded by Orlando Magic to the Milwaukee Bucks. Why did this happen?

J.J. Redick is just one example of basketball players with exemplary skills and a great college legacy that fail to deliver the expected performance on the NBA hardwood. There are also players that come to the NBA with little expectations and wow fans with stellar pomp and show, leading their teams to an NBA championship.

What leads to the success or disappointment of NBA players and teams? Being a basketball history buff that can talk basketball statistics back to the 1960's, I began collecting my thoughts on the subject. I studied profiles of several types of players, the progression of their NBA careers and factors that influenced their performance. Before long, I realized that surrounding factors play a huge role in making or breaking basketball teams. Some of the greatest players in NBA history are where they are because of who they had around them. I started documenting the facts and stories began to emerge. With these insights and analysis, I categorized these stories by player type, team dynamics, coaching style of the head coach and management style of the executive management. I played around with what-if scenarios and came up with recommendations for how to create and structure high performance NBA teams capable of winning championships. This book began to take shape.

This book is for elementary, middle and high school kids that play and follow basketball. This book is for college basketball players that are NBA hopefuls. This book is for every NBA player, NBA coach and NBA general manager. This book is for sports analysts, sports authors and writers who have a keen interest in basketball. This book is for all basketball fans and enthusiasts. For, I have a unique set of stories to tell. Stories that you will enjoy reading; stories that will help college basketball stars make their dream happen; stories that will provide insights to coaches and general managers on how to structure their NBA teams for success.

I sincerely hope you love the contents of this book as much as I do.

SHOOTING POINT GUARD

J immer Fredette was an amazing college basketball player. Playing 4 years at BYU, Jimmer became one of the best scorers in the nation. He could make shots from anywhere on the court, and in any situation: pulling up, shooting off the dribble, or even fading away with a defender's hand right in his face. In his senior year at BYU, Jimmer became one of college basketball's most electrifying players, scoring 29 points per game. When he went off, college basketball fans were attached to the TV. He was simply a pure shooter and an amazing scorer.

After his senior season, Jimmer was the 10th pick in the 2011 NBA draft, selected by the Milwaukee Bucks but traded to the Sacramento Kings. The hype for Jimmer in the NBA was crazy, especially with Kings fans. After years of unsuccessful seasons, Kings fans were hoping that Jimmer, alongside Kings all-star center, DeMarcus Cousins, could form one of the best duos in the NBA.

But Jimmer's 1st season with the Kings was disappointing. He scored only 7 points a game, while making only 38% of his shots. Kings fans were hoping for Jimmer to come back to his old self in his 2nd season with the Kings. But instead, there was more of the same. Jimmer, again, averaged 7 points per game. The next season, Jimmer was traded from the Kings, and his career went downhill from there.

Nobody really points a finger to what went wrong in Jimmer's career. But one thing is certain: Jimmer was a player with an unbelievable work ethic. Through college and in pro career, Jimmer has been one of the hardest working players. Jackson Emery, a former BYU player, has this to say about Jimmer: "One thing that I admire about Jimmer is the work ethic he has. I know a lot of people have doubted his ability, but Jimmer continues to shut down doubters and continues to work hard."

So we know Jimmer isn't one of those players who was a star in college and didn't succeed in the NBA because he didn't work hard enough. Jimmer also did not suffer any severe injuries. But maybe we can attribute his subpar performance to the pieces around him in Sacramento.

First, let's look at what a shooting point guard, like Jimmer, needs around him to succeed. First off, a shooting point guard needs to be his team's #1 scoring option. The point guard will have the ball in his hands, and make a majority of the decisions. By being the primary scoring option, the point guard will be able to create shots for himself while his teammates help by setting screens, acting as decoys and creating space. With this happening, the shooting point guard will get good, open shots.

Secondly, a shooting point guard needs a point forward. Now, a point forward is a forward who has point guard-like playmaking skills. These point forwards are good at finding their teammates open from the paint or inside the 3-point line. A point forward is very beneficial to a team because he can find outside shooters when the paint is clogged with defenders. Pairing an outside shooter with a point forward would be ideal, but this is especially true with an outside shooter who is a point guard. While an outside shooting guard will have the point guard to create shots for them, a shooting point guard needs a playmaker, and one from the post would be perfect.

Shooting 3-pointers over double teams is very hard. If the shooting point guard is the only one scoring on the offense, he will quickly get double-teamed. Forcing up contested shots is bad, but especially for an outside shooter. Forcing up ill-advised, outside shots can interrupt a player's rhythm and make their shot "cold" in no time. A player can start off the game by hitting four 3-point shots in a row. But he'll start getting double-teamed after that, and if he doesn't have good scorers to pass to, he'll force up shots. After missing 3 or 4 shots, the player will be out of his shooting rhythm, which is bad for any player. Even if this player is the best shooter in the world, it will take a few good and open shots for him to get back in his shooting flow.

When being double-teamed, a player's court vision is affected. Especially from behind the 3-point arc, it's hard for a player to complete a pass to the paint while being double-teamed. More likely than not, this type of pass would be a turnover. The better alternative would be to throw a short pass to the shooting guard, who will likely be also roaming the perimeter. Furthermore, the man who's guarding the shooting guard will likely be the one coming to double team the point guard (because he is the closest to the point guard), thus leaving the shooting guard wide open. Having a shooting guard who's a sharpshooter would make it much easier for the team and the point guard to produce effectively. It would be an easy pass for the point guard and an easy shot for the shooting guard.

Lastly, the point guard needs to play in a fast-paced offense. As mentioned earlier, a shooter needs to take many shots to get in his rhythm. More shot attempts equal more chances to score. A shooter can't be effective if he only takes 5-10 shots per game, as it takes about 5 good shots for a shooter to get in his rhythm. A good amount of shots for a shooter to take per game is 20-25, and maybe even more on a day where his shot is falling. Thus, to maximize the number of shots the shooting point guard gets, his team should play a fast style of basketball. And, we see a definite correlation between the type of centers and their team's style of play. Over the years, teams have started to play faster and take more shots. But as this has been happening, we've also seen the death of the "dominant-big, or one that is big and strong, but not very agile, a la Shaquille O'Neal. A dominant-big scores mostly while posting up, which takes up a lot of time. We can see that teams without a dominant-big play faster than the ones with a dominant-big. The first NBA team to really play fast was the "Run TMC" Warriors in the early 90's, who played a "Run 'N Gun" type of offense under head coach Don Nelson. Did they have a dominant-big man? Nope, not at all. Their center was 6'9 Tyrone Hill. To put this height into perspective, Magic Johnson, a point guard, is 6'9. Hill may have been undersized at the center position, but he made up for it with his speed.

Shooting point guards are a new breed in the NBA. Many point guards are either pass-first or athletic slashers. Mark Price, who played for the Cleveland Cavaliers in the early nineties, was an amazing shooter at the point guard position. However, he was also a pass-first player, and never averaged more than 20 points per game. Another point guard, who may end up as the GREATEST shooter of all time, is Stephen Curry. Steph and Jimmer are actually very similar players. If we replace Steph with Jimmer on the Warriors and put Steph on the Kings for 3 seasons, maybe Jimmer would be the 2-time MVP instead of Steph. I am saying this because the pieces around Stephen Curry compliment him PERFECTLY.

Steph has something Jimmer didn't have: a point forward in Draymond Green. Green averaged 7 assists in 2016/17 season, which is quite a bit for a point forward. Green is a pass-first player, which is very rare for a power forward. Combine his passing with his excellent rebounding skills, and Green creates MANY open looks for Curry and the rest of the Warriors. Green can get a defensive rebound and quickly spot a Warrior running in transition for an easy basket. Or, he can get an offensive rebound, and kick it out to Curry (or Klay Thompson) for an easy 3-pointer. Because most of the defense would be collapsed in the paint trying to grab the rebound, a 3-point shot would be wide open.

Klay Thompson is a shooting guard who is another excellent shooter. Klay and Steph are called the "Splash Brothers" because they're the 2 best shooters in the NBA on the same team. Curry rarely takes 3s when double-teamed because he'll often have Thompson open. But in recent years, Thompson has become such a shooting threat that defenses are reluctant to double-team Curry at the cost of leaving Klay open. Good shooters like Curry and Thompson are able to consistently hit 3s with opponent's hands in their face, giving them a good chance to make a shot unless they're double-teamed. And if they do get double-teamed, they can find the other "Splash Brother" for a WIDE open 3. This is what makes the Warriors unstoppable.

Lastly, the Warriors play a fast brand of basketball, which maximizes the number of shots that Curry gets. In their small-ball or "Death" lineup, Green plays center.

Green rarely posts up and is faster than any center in the NBA. When the Warriors use their "Death" lineup, Steph gets the maximum amount of shots.

Did Jimmer have these pieces around him during his rookie year in Sacramento? Not at all. In fact, he had quite the opposite. First off, the Kings had no point forward. This meant instead of focusing on scoring, Jimmer had to be the team's main playmaker, focusing on distributing the ball to Tyreke Evans and center Demarcus Cousins. The Kings already had 2010 Rookie of the Year, Tyreke Evans, as one of their go-to scorers. But Evans was a slasher who scored when driving to the hoop, not shooting from outside. Furthermore, Evans had poor playmaking abilities and often took heavily contested layups rather than passing to the open man. DeMarcus Cousins was the Kings' best player. But Cousins was a dominant player who scored by posting up. With most of the Kings' possessions including a Cousins post up, the Kings played a slow brand of basketball. And with Evans and Cousins taking a majority of the shots, Jimmer only attempted 7 shots per game. And there wasn't a good playmaker to get Fredette a good shot: a lot of the shots he took were contested.

An ideal situation for Jimmer would have been a draft to a team that believed in him so much that they built their team around him. Ray Allen, arguably the greatest 3-point shooter in NBA history, was getting older. The Boston Celtics were shopping him on the market as it was unlikely that he would stay in Boston for much longer. With Ray Allen being a sharpshooter, he would have been a good player to pair with Jimmer. Pau Gasol, one of the key pieces to the Lakers' championship teams in the late 2000s, was also being shopped at that time. He was even traded for Chris Paul in a deal that got vetoed by the then NBA commissioner David Stern. Pau Gasol is one of the best passing big men and plays well in a fast paced offense. With this, Jimmer would have had all the pieces around him to succeed. He would have had a point forward in Gasol, a sharpshooter in Ray Allen and a team that could play fast to maximize the number of shots he gets.

2

PLAYMAKING POINT GUARD

I f you were a fan of the NBA in the late 2000s, you probably knew who Rajon Rondo was. And you probably either loved him for his tenacity and hustle or hated him for his aggressiveness from the point guard position. However, love him or hate him, there's no denying the fact that Rajon Rondo was one of the best point guards in the league. In addition to his on-court hustle, incredible basketball IQ, and court vision, he also had a marvelous ability to play physical defense and get tons of steals.

Rondo played his first 7 years in the NBA with the Celtics. He was drafted with the 21st pick of the 2006 NBA draft by the Phoenix Suns, but was traded to the Boston Celtics. After having an average rookie season, Rondo became the Celtics starting point guard for the 2007-2008 season. But promoting Rondo to starting point guard wasn't the only move the Celtics made in the 2007 offseason. The Celtics acquired Kevin Garnett and Ray Allen: two of the best players in the NBA at that time. Garnett and Allen, along with Celtics superstar Paul Pierce, formed a much anticipated Big 3. The team won the 2008 NBA finals but never won a championship after that. Pierce, Garnett and Allen were all in their 30's when the Celtics won the 2008 championship and were definitely past their peak. In 2010, Pierce was 33, Garnett was 34, and Ray Allen was 35. But, despite their "old age" and declining athleticism, the Celtics still managed to make the NBA finals and push the Lakers to 7 games.

One of the major reasons why the aging Celtics were able to make the finals in 2010 was the play of Rajon Rondo. Rondo had developed into one of the top two-way players in the NBA. He was part of the NBA's All-Defensive 1st team, and lead the league in steals. On offense, Rondo was one of the league's top playmakers, and averaged nearly 10 assists per game to go with 14 points per game. Rondo was recognized for this as he was named to his first ever All-Star team in 2010. But his individual success would continue.

Rondo averaged more than 11 assists per game for each of the next 3 seasons, and led the league in assists during the 2012 and 2013 season. He started to mold into one of the best point guards in the NBA, as he was arguably the best passer and perimeter defender in the league. Rondo would become the leader of the Celtics in 2012, as Garnett, Allen, and Piece were all older than 35 years.

But, as the Big 3 were aging, the Celtics thought it was time to let go of them and start rebuilding. The Celtics let Ray Allen leave for the Heat in 2012, and traded Garnett and Pierce to the Nets in the summer of 2013. Rajon Rondo was the only member from the Celtics championship core still on the team. And even his time in Boston was coming to a close, as the Celtics were looking to get rid of him and form a completely new team. Rondo was traded to the Mavericks in December of 2013. And, after making 4 straight all-star games with the Celtics (2010, 2011, 2012, and 2013), Rondo wouldn't make another one after being traded from Boston. He went from arguably the best point guard in the NBA to an average starter.

Why did Rondo go from a superstar with the Celtics to an average player with the Mavericks, Kings, and Bulls? Rondo went from the best passer in the NBA to a somewhat average one. Why? Well, let's first see what a pass-first point guard needs around him to succeed.

Pass-first point guards have slowly been diminishing, as there are few of them in today's NBA. A pass-first point guard is a player who is more likely to pass than shoot. These types of players can score the basketball, but often pass up good shots for a better shot for their teammate.

First off, and most importantly, a pass-first point guard needs teammates who can score the basketball. Having teammates who can score is important for many reasons, but none more important than the effect it has on the point guards mindset. For a playmaking point guard to be good, he has to go out on the court excited to make something happen, not just getting the ball in the basket himself, but by setting up one of his teammates to score. And for a play-maker, this mindset isn't a one-game deal. It's the mindset a playmaker goes out and plays with for his entire career. And a playmaking point guard is at his absolute best when he's fully locked in with the passing mindset. For this to happen, the playmaker has to be fully invested and has to have full belief in his teammates. Remember, a playmaker is someone who passes up a good shot for himself, hoping that his teammate will be able to convert to an even better shot. This will only happen if a playmaker has full belief that his teammates can easily convert: not once or twice, but time after time, on the good shots they're set up with.

So we know that playmaking point guards need to be

playing alongside good scorers to be the most effective. The question we need to ask, however, is what type of scorers should a playmaker be playing with? Putting a playmaker alongside an isolation scorer or a slasher (such as Dwayne Wade or Kobe Bryant) wouldn't allow the point guard to have a huge impact. A playmaker is best when he has teammates who are best when scoring off the catch or with one or two dribbles.

The playmaker's main passing option should be an athletic forward, a power forward who is athletic and one who can score the ball with ease near the hoop. These players are able to convert on shots near the basket thanks to their high jumping abilities. Playing alongside an athletic forward is practically a playmaker's dream; he has a player who he can find near the basket knowing they will make a play. Not all of these forwards have to have extraordinary athleticism; they can make up for it with good moves near the basket, as well as a strong midrange jumper.

But an athletic forward isn't all a good playmaker needs around him to succeed. If the point guard doesn't have options, and keeps passing to the athletic forward, plays become predictable resulting in many turnovers. So, who else can a playmaking point guard play alongside with to be the most effective? Well, they already have an inside scorer. When the defense collapses on the inside to stop the athletic forward, it's nice to have some backup on the perimeter. Thus, it's essential that along with an athletic forward, a playmaking point guard should play with a perimeter shooter. A perimeter shooter is a player who is best when shooting off the catch or with one or two dribbles. These type of players, as I mentioned earlier, are the best type of players to pair a playmaking point guard with.

Almost all of the best passers in NBA history have had

these pieces around them. Let's start with John Stockton, the NBA's all-time leader in career assists. Stockton finished his career with 15,806 assists. But he didn't do this by himself. He played alongside Karl Malone, one of the greatest scorers ever. Malone, a power forward, finished his career with 36,928 points: the 2nd most ever! Stockton and Malone formed an amazing duo. Malone was such a good scorer, not only because of his athleticism but also because of his inside scoring moves and his midrange jump shot. But Stockton and Malone didn't win by themselves, complementing the historic duo was Jeff Hornacek. Hornacek was one of the best shooters in the '90s.

While John Stockton is the NBA's all-time leader in career assists, he is 2nd on the list for career assist per game average. Who's 1st on that list? Magic Johnson. Magic is regarded as one of the 5 greatest players in NBA history, largely because of his extraordinary passing ability. Magic played on some of the greatest teams in NBA history. The 80s Lakers were stacked with talent, as they won 5 NBA championships that decade. But Magic wouldn't have been the passer he was without playing alongside the teammates he had. Kareem Abdul-Jabbar was like an athletic forward, except he was 7'2 and played center. But Kareem was very athletic and played like an athletic forward. He is the NBA's all-time leading scorer, having scored 38,387 points throughout his career. But it wasn't just Magic and Kareem who led the Lakers to 5 championships in the 80s. Byron Scott was a sharpshooter and one of the best 3 point shooters of that time. Magic was able to rack up tons of assists playing alongside Kareem, Scott, and some other great players.

These guys did great in the 80s and 90s, but the 2000s had some great playmakers too. Steve Nash hit his peak when playing for the Phoenix Suns in 2005. He averaged 11.5 assists that year and won the MVP award. He would go on to average double-digit assists for 6 of the next 7 seasons. This is because he had great players around him that complimented him very well. He had an athletic forward in Amare Stoudemire. Amare was one of the best bigs in the game, he had an array of moves near the basket and could score with ease. In 2005, when Nash won the MVP, Amare averaged 26 points per game! But Nash also had a sharpshooter in Raja Bell. Bell was a great shooter who would almost always cash in on open shot attempts. In the 2006 NBA season, when Nash won his 2nd MVP award, Bell shot 44% from behind the arc and averaged 14 points per game.

So we know now what playmakers need around them. Let's look at Rajon Rondo's career to see which players he had when.

Rondo was at the peak of his career when he was playing alongside the Celtics Big 3. Who was part of the Big 3? Kevin Garnett, an athletic forward and arguably, the greatest power forward to play the game, as well as Paul Pierce and Ray Allen, two of the best 3 point shooters EVER! Not much needs to be said about these 3 guys; they made it easy for Rondo to rack up assists. Each one could consistently score 18 or more points on any given night, and many of their shots came of off passes by Rondo.

Did he have these pieces when he got traded to Dallas? No. Dirk Nowitzki could score as a power forward, but he had no athleticism. And Dirk, even while playing power forward, was the best shooter on the Mavs!

3

PERIMETER SHOOTER

J Redick is one of the greatest players in college basketball history. Playing at Duke in 2006, JJ won the 2006 National College Player Of The Year award. He is Duke's all-time leader in points, as well as 3-pointers.

JJ Redick was, and still is, an amazing shooter. He can knock down shots from anywhere. He has excellent shooting form and gets a great amount of lift from his legs so he can have a good chance of making every shot he takes. JJ averaged 27 points per game in his senior season at Duke, while shooting 42% from 3. His 3-point shooting, combined with his basketball IQ, made him a lottery pick in the 2006 NBA draft.

Redick was the 13th pick in that year's draft, selected by the Orlando Magic. Though he was an excellent shooter and had great basketball IQ, he was not very fast and lacked skills on defense. But JJ went from averaging 27 points per game at Duke to averaging no more than 10 points per game for the next 4 seasons.

How could this have happened? JJ is a starter in the NBA

now, but he spent his true prime as a role player on the Magic. JJ's poor play in his prime years with the Magic wasn't completely his fault. Why?

Because, there are some players with certain strengths and tendencies that a perimeter scorer, like JJ, need around him to be successful. First off and most importantly, the scorer needs the ball. The scorer needs to be the go-to guy on his team and needs to take the most shots on his team. This doesn't mean that he should be surrounded by guys who can't make shots, but pairing a scorer with another ball dominant player who is a shoot-first player isn't ideal.

Secondly, a perimeter scorer needs a pass-first point guard alongside him in the backcourt. This pass-first player has to be fine with taking fewer shots for the good of the team. Many have described a great pass-first player as someone who would "pass up a good shot for a great shot." Having a great passer alongside a perimeter scorer is ideal for a few reasons. First, this ensures that the perimeter scorer will get most of the scoring opportunities from behind the arc, as the point guard won't be taking as many shots. Secondly, the perimeter scorer doesn't have to create a shot for himself all the time; he can rely on the point guard to get him the ball in good position to score.

Thirdly, a perimeter scorer needs a forward who is a great defender and unselfish. Having a forward who could guard all positions would take a lot of pressure off the perimeter scorer on defense. The best scorer on most teams is their shooting guard, and having the perimeter scorer guarding the opposition's best scorer would indeed tire him out. Having a forward who can lock the opposition's best scorer down would save tons of energy for the perimeter scorer, allowing him to take shots on the offensive end. On the offensive end of the floor, having a forward who is unselfish, often classified as a "point forward", a forward who plays like a point guard, would result in more good shots from the perimeter scorer. You will notice I said good shots. Good playmakers are able to find their teammates for high percentage and open shots. Playing alongside two play-makers would result in the perimeter scorer getting many good shots, and easily knocking them down.

Lastly, a perimeter scorer needs a big man/center that can rebound the ball and is fast and versatile. Rebounds are critical in the game of basketball; more rebounds mean more chances to score. Having a center who can grab rebounds, especially offensive ones, gives the perimeter scorer more chances to score. The big also has to be fast and able to score in many ways. A big man who can't score the basketball isn't one that should be playing good minutes in the NBA, especially when a size advantage is there. The big man should be easily scoring point after point on the smaller defender. But *how* the big man scores is very impor-tant. Having a big man, who is able to score off cuts, pick and rolls, mid-range jump shots and in transition would save a lot of time on the offensive end. Pairing a perimeter scorer with a big who usually scores while posting up is a bad combination. Post-ups usually take up a huge chunk of the clock and really slow the game down, lessening the number of shots the perimeter scorer would get. Instead, pairing a perimeter scorer who can rack up points in other, faster ways would keep the game going at an ideal pace, and would allow the perimeter scorer to get a good amount of shots in.

We've seen many successful shooting guards play very well with these people around them. Let's start with Reggie Miller, arguably the greatest shooter in NBA history. As players, Reggie and JJ were very similar and could shoot from anywhere, in any situation. In fact, some can say that JJ had the potential to be even better than Reggie because of his basketball IQ. But Reggie's production was maximized due to the pieces around him. He had the most important thing: the ball. In his entire 18 year career playing for the Indiana Pacers, Reggie was always the #1 scoring option. He played alongside Mark Jackson, one of the greatest passers in NBA history. Jackson ranks 4th in all-time career assists: only behind Steve Nash, Jason Kidd and John Stockton. But Jackson wasn't the only good playmaker on the team. Starting at the forward spot was Derrick McKey, an unselfish player who had a knack for passing. But McKey's main strengths were on the defensive end. At 6'10", McKey could guard all five positions. He was named to the NBA's All-Defensive 2nd Team twice. At center was the 7'4" Rik Smits, a solid rebounder who was a versatile scorer. Smits was also surprisingly versatile, allowing him to be effective on the offensive and defensive ends of the floor.

Michael Jordan, another perimeter scorer, is considered to be the greatest basketball player of all time. But he was put into a perfect situation with the Chicago Bulls, as Jordan's teammates fit him perfectly. Let's analyze the latter half of Jordan's career: when he was more of a perimeter scorer and less of an explosive athletic freak always driving to the basket. Like JJ, Jordan wasn't athletic (in the latter half of his career) but had a great mind for basketball. Jordan's consistent jumper allowed him to play at a high level until he was 40. Most of his late-career success came between 1996 and 1998: where Jordan and the Bulls won 203 out of 246 regular season games. The Bulls also won championships those 3 years.

Complementing Jordan in the backcourt was Ron Harper. Harper wasn't the best playmaker, but he played good defense and was excellent at getting Jordan the ball when he needed it. Harper was often a team's go-to scorer in his prime, when he played for the Clippers and Cavaliers. But he changed his game when traded to the Bulls, which hugely benefited Jordan's production. At forward was Scottie Pippen, arguably the greatest defensive player of all time. Pippen ALWAYS guarded the other team's best player and simply shut him down. He forced an absurd amount of turnovers and got a huge amount of steals, leading to many easy fastbreak buckets for Jordan and the Bulls. Though he didn't play center, Dennis Rodman was the biggest contributor to the Bulls frontcourt. Though he was undersized as a 6'7 power forward, Rodman did not let that stop him from grabbing rebounds. Rodman led the NBA in rebounding for 7 years in a row; this was a tremendous contribution to Jordan's success. More rebounds lead to more shots.

With all of this, Jordan had a lot of playing time during the Bulls' championship runs. The key thing that Redick didn't have in Orlando was playing time. For his entire tenure playing for the Magic (6 years), he was always either the backup or 3rd string shooting guard.

Why was this? There was always another shooting guard which fit better with the starting lineup than Redick did. The Magic's starting lineup stayed consistent while JJ was in Orlando. Jameer Nelson was the starter at point guard for 5 out of the 6 years. Dwight Howard started at center for all the 6 years. Hedo Turkoglu was the starting small forward for 5 out of the 6 years. Though the starting power forward wasn't the same all 6 years, it was always a stretch 4, either Ryan Anderson or Rashard Lewis.

So we have Jameer Nelson, a scoring, shoot-first point guard. At small forward is Hedo Turkoglu, a playmaking "point forward". At the power forward position was, as I mentioned earlier, a stretch 4, or a big man that shoots long-range shots. At center was Dwight Howard, who was, at the time, one of the best players in the NBA.

So the Magic had their offense figured out. They had 3 scorers (Nelson, Lewis, and Howard) and an unselfish forward to get them the ball (Turkoglu). Remember, there is only one ball. Instead of putting Redick, a 3 point shooter and scorer, in the lineup, the Magic decided they needed a perimeter defender. Thus, Courtney Lee, a good perimeter defender, started at the shooting guard spot instead of Redick.

The ideal situation for Redick was if the Magic didn't take him in with the 12th pick. Instead, they could've picked Rajon Rondo, a pass-first point guard with excellent perimeter defending skills. Rondo could've been the starting point guard for the Magic, with Nelson sliding down to the shooting guard position.

Redick, meanwhile, could have been selected by the Utah Jazz. The Jazz had barely any shooting guards in the 2006-2007 season (Redick's rookie year), thus point guard Deron Williams had to play shooting guard. Deron Williams was a pass-first point guard who only scored when he needed to. With Redick on the Jazz, he'd have all the pieces around him to succeed. He'd have a pass-first point guard in Williams, an unselfish defensive small forward in Andrei Kirilenko, and a rebounding versatile scorer in Carlos Boozer.

4

SLASHER

N ow, Evan Turner wasn't necessarily a huge star in college. But he was an all-around, excellent player, which is what college scouts took notice of while watching Ohio State play in the 2009-2010 college basketball season. That was Turner's junior year, and he averaged 20 points, 9 rebounds, and 6 assists. Standing at 6'7 and having almost a 7'0 wingspan, Turner had great size and length to make plays on both the defensive and offensive end. His ball-handling abilities were as good as those of a point guard. Turner had great passing skills too. His court vision, combined with his smarts and shot IQ allowed him to find an open man when the defense collapsed on him in the paint.

But what made Turner such a good player and attracting draft prospect, was his ability to drive to the basket and finish inside. Turner's athleticism never stood out. Turner was faster than average but definitely not a freak athlete. But Turner used more than just speed to get to the basket. His ball-handling abilities and feel of comfort with the ball was definitely an advantage for Turner. He used the crossover and many other moves to change direction and get the defense off balance, thus giving him an open lane to drive to the hoop. Turner had GREAT upper body strength, which allowed him to absorb contact while slashing to the hoop and making plays near the basket. He was also a very strong finisher. He was very smart in using his body to shield the ball from the defender and had an array of moves to finish with contact or over a bigger defender. Though Turner lacked a great jump shot, many scouts thought that Turner was so good at attacking the basket that he wouldn't need to take jumpers in the NBA.

Turner was cut out to be one of the best slashers the NBA had ever seen. Many thought he could mold into a Dwyane Wade/prime Kobe Bryant. But Turner never relied on his athleticism, which gave him the potential to be an elite slasher for his entire career, even when he loses his athleticism.

So we can all see that Evan Turner was a special player, definitely capable of being an NBA superstar. He was drafted by the Philadelphia 76ers with the 2nd pick of the 2010 NBA draft. 76ers fans imagined a bright future for Turner and the Sixers.

While the Sixers would make the playoffs for the next 2 seasons, Turner never lived up to expectations. He averaged 7 points per game in his rookie year, 9 points per game in his 2nd season, and 13 in his 3rd season. To put this into perspective, Dwyane Wade, another slasher, averaged 27 points per game in his 3rd season in the league. Evan Turner was 24 during his 3rd season. When Kobe Bryant, also a slasher and one of the greatest of all time was 24, he averaged 30 points per game.

Then, in the 2013 offseason, the Sixers made some huge changes to the roster. They traded away or released most of their core, leaving Turner as the only starter from the 2012-2013 season remaining for the 2013-2014 season. Surrounded by many young players, Turner took control of the team and emerged to what seemed like the best season of his career, as he averaged 18 points per game in the first 54 games of the season. But the Sixers wanted to rebuild and decided to trade Turner to the Pacers in the middle of the season. Turner only averaged 7 points per game for the Pacers in the rest of the season.

Turner never lost his ability to play well, as he averaged 18 points per game for a good chunk of the 2013-2014 season. His team and the players surrounding him really changed before that season, so we could possibly attribute Turner's short stint of success to the players around him and how they somewhat fit what he, as a slasher, needed around him to succeed.

What does a slasher need around him to succeed? Obviously, a slasher needs the ball in his hands often and needs to be his team's 1st or second scoring option. There needs to be possessions where the slasher's teammates can clear out and let the slasher take the whole possession to himself.

But what many may not know is that pairing a slasher with a dominant big man actually works perfectly. A dominant big man usually can't be stopped with one defender, as he is too big and strong. Thus, the big man will often cause two or even three defenders to leave their man to double team or triple team the dominant big. With most of the defense collapsed where the dominant big is, the opposite side of the floor would have a wide open lane for the slasher to drive. For example, let's say a dominant big man is posting up on the left block. He will attract a defensive player to come double team, and another defensive player to stay near the dominant big in help defense. Now, you have three defenders collapsed around the left block trying to stop the big. Now, you have only two defenders guarding the right side of the floor. This will likely leave gaps for the slasher to penetrate to the basket.

But how can we ensure an open lane or gaps for the slasher to drive? It has to do with the other three players on the floor, the point guard and the two forwards. To ensure an open lane for the slasher, these three players have to be perimeter threats or at least be able to consistently knock down open 3s. Thus, the defenders will always have an eye on the perimeter, not wanting to give up any open 3s, and will not be focused on closing the gaps and not letting the slasher drive.

How can this situation work out? Well, we already have the dominant big at the left block, attracting two or three defenders to stop him. Both forwards will slide to the corners, ready for the ball to hit an open 3. The big will likely kick the ball out to the right corner because there will be less defense on that side of the floor. One of the weak side defenders will immediately close out on the right corner, trying to stop the 3-point shot. While the rest of the defense will be expecting a 3-pointer, and thus will try to box out the dominant big to get the rebound, a lane would be wide open for the slasher to drive. The forward at the right corner could quickly swing the ball to the right wing, where the slasher would be. The slasher would immediately take off to the hoop. Though defenders could try to stop him near the free-throw line, more likely than not in this type of situation, the slasher would get to the paint without being touched by the defender.

Some of the greatest slashers in NBA history have had these pieces around them which allowed them to succeed. Let's start off with Dwyane Wade. Dwyane Wade in his

prime was arguably the best slasher in the NBA. In just his
3rd season in the NBA (2005-2006), Wade averaged 27 points
per game and led the Heat to their 1st ever NBA championship. Wade didn't do this by himself, though. At center
was Shaquille O'Neal, the most dominant NBA player of all-
time. Now, Shaq may have been 34, but he was still the same
player. "Shaq" and "D-Wade" were also surrounded by
many shooters: Gary Payton, Antoine Walker, Jason Kapono,
and James Posey were all huge perimeter threats. All of this
led to a very efficient season for Dwyane Wade, as he averaged 9 shot attempts in the paint per game and made 61%
of them.

Another great slasher is Kobe Bryant. Now, many may
remember Kobe as more of a perimeter player than a
slasher in recent years, but Kobe definitely was a slasher in
his prime. And, just like Dwyane Wade, Kobe played alongside Shaquille O'Neal, the most dominant player of all time.
But this Shaquille O'Neal was at his peak, as he had won the
NBA MVP in 2000. Around Kobe and Shaq were many
shooters: Rick Fox, Robert Horry, and Derek Fisher. These
pieces around Kobe made him emerge as one of the NBA's
top young players in the early 2000's.

Did Evan Turner have these pieces around him? Not at
all. In Turner's first three years in Philly, the Sixers made the
playoffs ⅔ seasons, but the pieces around him didn't compliment Turner. Let's start with the Sixers center, Spencer
Hawes. Hawes was the opposite of dominant: he rarely even
scored in double-digits, let alone attract double teams. The
Sixers were a slashing team and barely had any shooters.
Their point guard, Jrue Holiday, was a shoot-first point
guard.

Here's what the Sixers could've done differently to build
their team around Turner. They had good seasons in 2011

and 2012 and changes only started happening in 2013. But with those changes, the Sixers should've built their team around Turner. They could've signed Dwight Howard in the 2013 summer. Howard is the closest to Shaq in terms of sheer dominance at the center positions. Surround Turner with shooters, and you've brought him a bright future.

5

SCORING SMALL FORWARD

Michael Beasley was simply a superstar in college. Playing for Kansas State, Beasley averaged 26 points and 12 rebounds a game, while shooting 53% from the field. He decided to enter the 2008 NBA draft after his freshman year in college. Prior to the draft, Beasley was ranked as the best player in the draft, even ahead of future league MVPs Russell Westbrook and Derrick Rose, as well as future all-stars Kevin Love and Brook Lopez. Yes, there was a lot of hype surrounding Beasley. He was a scoring machine at the small forward position. He was athletically gifted and had all the makings of a future superstar.

Derrick Rose was selected to his hometown Bulls with the 1st pick of the draft. The Miami Heat had the 2nd pick of the draft, which they used to select Beasley. Michael Beasley dominated the NBA Summer League (league in the offseason for rookies and 2nd year players) which left no doubt in everyone's mind that Beasley would be a future star. At the time Celtics coach Doc Rivers said, "Offensively, I've been a big believer in him, I just think he can score. I think one day he may lead the league in scoring. He has a Carmelo Anthony ability to score the ball. He's a matchup problem every night; he has quickness and a shot at that size. That makes him tough to guard."

Beasley never played horrible: he averaged 14 points in his 1st year in the NBA and 15 in his 2nd. But he never reached his full offensive potential of leading the league in scoring. The closest he got to his potential was in 2011 after he was traded from the Heat to the Timberwolves for future draft picks. This trade by the Heat was meant to clear up cap space to sign LeBron James and Chris Bosh, and re-sign Dwyane Wade. On the Timberwolves, Beasley averaged 19.2 points per game in the 2010-2011 season. But that would be Beasley's peak. After 2011, Beasley averaged no more than 13 points per game.

Michael Beasley hasn't had a horrible NBA career but definitely didn't reach his full potential. He was supposed to be an NBA superstar, but ended up as an average starter, able to score double digits on any given night but not able to do more than that. But the real question is: was he given a fair chance to do more than 10 points per game? Did the pieces around him compliment him well enough so he could reach his full potential?

Well, let's first look at what a scoring small forward should have around him to succeed. First off, a scoring small forward needs the ball a decent amount. The player should get the ball often, but not too much. Remember, this is a forward who will rarely bring the ball down the court or receive it much behind the 3-point line. A forward can receive the ball anywhere from the wings (free-throw line extended), to the elbows (corners of the free-throw line), to even the painted area. There will be many defensive players in this area of the court, which could lead them to possibly use 2 to 3 players to deny the ball from the scoring small forward. If the scoring small forward gets the ball (and does something with it) every possession, the defense will eventually crowd the player, not letting him get the ball. The times he will get the ball, he'll be smothered by 2 to 3 players. And while a point guard or shooting guard can use their speed and playmaking abilities to beat double or triple teams, a forward or center is essentially trapped.

Thus, pairing an athletic point guard who can score and pass with this scoring forward would be ideal. This way, the scoring forward would get the ball a decent amount, but not at the rate when he's denied and doubled every time he touches the ball. This point guard should be able to have the speed to easily drive to the basket and the scoring abilities to where he attracts attention away from the scoring forward, or even possibly double teams. This will result in the scoring forward getting the ball with only one man to beat, rather than 2 or 3. Point guard should have good playmaking skills, so he'll be able to find the scoring forward in good scoring situations.

Alongside the scoring forward and point guard on offense, there should be few perimeter shooters capable of drilling shots from behind the arc when needed. This will attract defenders to the perimeter to prevent these 3-point shots, allowing the scoring forward to get good scoring opportunities inside the 3-point line.

While the scoring forward should be making contributions on the defensive end of the floor, he should be using more of his energy on the offensive end of the floor. The scoring forward should be able to rest on defense from time to time and not be harmed. Thus, it's essential to pair the scoring small forward with a good perimeter defender and low post defender. Thus, instead of having to guard man-to-man on the primary ball handler(s) or post player(s), he can take a backseat and conserve his energy by playing help defense of off-ball man defense.

Some successful scoring small forwards include Kevin Durant and Carmelo Anthony. These guys were, at their peak, complemented perfectly with an athletic point guard, shooters, and defenders.

Let's start with Kevin Durant, and his 2013-2014 MVP season where he averaged 32 points per game. His point guard was future NBA MVP Russell Westbrook. Westbrook was (and still is) the 2nd most athletic player in the game. His speed combined with his aggressiveness allowed him to drive to the basket with ease. Russ had an array of finishing moves he could use near the basket, which made him an inside scoring threat (as he averaged 22 points per game that year). When the defense collapsed on him, he could kick the ball out to Durant for a good shot.

Russ and KD were also surrounded by great perimeter shooters: Caron Butler, Jeremy Lamb, and Derek Fisher. The defense often closed out on them, not allowing them to get off a shot. But that cleared space for KD inside the 3-point line, allowing him to penetrate to the basket.

On defense, Durant was surrounded by Thabo Sefolosha, one of the best perimeter defenders, and Serge Ibaka, one of the league's best low post defenders. This allowed Durant to take a few defensive possessions off, allowing him to save his energy to score on offense.

Another great scoring forward is Carmelo Anthony. Carmelo's best season came in 2006-2007 when he averaged 29 points per game. Like KD played alongside Russell Westbrook, 'Melo played alongside another great point guard, Allen Iverson. Iverson was the 2001 MVP and was 31 in the 2006-2007 season. But he was still athletic and had a lethal crossover which allowed him to drive to the basket with ease. Iverson was a great scorer, as he had averaged a career high 33 points per game the year before while playing for the Sixers. Iverson was definitely a feared scorer that year: as feared as Carmelo. But Iverson decided to take a backseat in scoring, and dished the ball to 'Melo whenever he could. The Nuggets also had great perimeter shooters in Steve Blake and JR Smith. These were guys who Carmelo could kick the ball out to for perimeter shots. Once the defense started closing out on them, Carmelo would have space to score inside. On defense, JR Smith was a lockdown perimeter defender, and Marcus Camby was considered the best low post defender.

Did Beasley ever have this? Not at all. In Miami, Beasley was the 2nd scoring option. But the 1st was Dwyane Wade: one of the best players in the NBA. While Beasley was on the Heat, Wade averaged 28.4 points per game (over 2 seasons, 2008-2009 and 2009-2010). In Beasley's rookie year, Wade averaged 30.2 points per game, which led the league. Wade was the Heat's go-to option on offense and took a vast majority of the shots. In Beasley's 2010-11 season with Minnesota, averaging a career-high 19 points per game, he was still the 2nd scoring option behind Kevin Love (even though he took more shots than Love). And even when Beasley had the ball enough to score a decent amount, the pieces around him didn't compliment him at all.

Beasley did play alongside another scoring threat. But instead of that scoring threat being a playmaking point guard, it was another scoring forward, Kevin Love. Love's and Beasley's games were quite different: Beasley was more athletic and Love was stronger down low. While both play-ers' outside games were very similar, Beasley scored inside while slashing. Love, on the other hand, scored inside by posting up.

So already, we have Love clogging up the paint. Love was not a good passer out of the post: he only averaged 2.5 assists per game that year. And to make matters worse, teammate Luke Ridnour was a shoot-first point guard. He led his team in assists with five per game. But with Beasley, Love, and Wesley Johnson, a good playmaker would be racking up at least 8 assists per game on the Timberwolves.

Wesley Johnson played at shooting guard for the Wolves, but he was more of a slasher than a shooter. Love, at the time, was definitely more of an inside scorer than an outside. He could shoot the ball, but only took two 3 point shots per game.

With Love and Johnson attracting defense to the paint, Beasley still managed to score off of mid-range jumpers. He shot 543 mid-range shots that year, and made 40% of them. He didn't get too many shots in the paint (254) or restricted area (285) but converted on most of them.

The next year, Minnesota signed Nikola Pekovic and Ricky Rubio (drafted by the Timberwolves in '09 but played in Spain until 2011). Though Rubio was a GREAT playmaker, Pekovic was a ball-dominant, post-up scorer (averaged 13 points per game that year). Love had added more scoring moves to his game, and averaged 26 points per game that season. With Love, Pekovic, Ridnour, Johnson, and Rubio taking most of the shots, the ball rarely got to Beasley. His production significantly dropped, leading the Timberwolves to demote him from the starting small forward to Wesley Johnson's backup.

Looking back on it, the Heat shouldn't have selected Michael Beasley. Yes, Beasley may have been the best player in the draft, but he was simply a scoring machine. The Heat already had Dwyane Wade: a scoring machine himself who was at the peak of his career. Pairing a rookie scoring machine with another superstar scoring machine decreased the rookie's production, which essentially affected the rookie's mindset and lowered his confidence.

The ideal situation (for Beasley) would have been the Heat picking Russell Westbrook, a point guard who they know would work well with Wade. Now, the Minnesota Timberwolves had the 3rd pick in the draft. They ended up taking OJ Mayo and trading him, along with Antoine Walker and a few other players to the Memphis Grizzlies for Kevin Love, Mike Miller, Jason Collins and Brian Cardinal. In this situation, if Minnesota would have taken Beasley with the #3 pick, he would've had teammate Sebastian Telfair, an athletic point guard and a poor man's Russell Westbrook. Beasley would have been paired with shooters Randy Foye and Corey Brewer. Down low would've been Al Jefferson, one of the best low post defenders in the NBA. This would've provided Beasley with good pieces around him.

6

STRETCH 4

Troy Murphy was simply "the man" in college. Playing 3 years at Notre Dame, Murphy averaged 21 points, 10 rebounds, and shot nearly 50% from the floor. Murphy, standing at 6'11 played power forward and center. But, unlike most centers, Murphy could shoot the basketball.

Boy, could he shoot. Murphy was an "assassin" from deep. His shooting stroke was unlike any, with fluidity in his shot which was like no other big men. With his high shooting arc and incredible height, Murphy could shoot long range jumpers while being limitedly contested by defenders.

But no big man can play college level division 1 basketball with only shooting skills. For Murphy, as a big man, his 3 point shooting was just a weapon he could use. Murphy had a great inside scoring game, as he was tall. Though not very aggressive, Murphy could still score easily inside because of his array of post moves. Murphy's mid-range game was also exceptionally good. He was deadly from around both elbows, with one side being as feared as the other.

Murphy, however, wasn't very athletic. He lacked lateral quickness and high jumping ability, but he made up for it with his incredible basketball IQ, which was becoming lethal in the power forward and big man positions. The basketball IQ that he possessed allowed him to find his teammates open from the post.

When Murphy entered the 2001 NBA draft, nobody really knew where Murphy would end up. Some thought he could be a top 3 pick, because of the incredible shooting skills he had from the power forward position. As a scoring machine with a high basketball IQ, some scouts thought Murphy was the gold in the 2001 NBA draft. Others thought that Murphy, lacking aggressiveness inside and heavily relying on his outside shot, wasn't a true big man. With his defense under par, some scouts thought Murphy wasn't at all a complete player and said that he shouldn't even be a lottery pick.

Murphy ended up being a lottery pick, barely. He was the 14th pick in the 2001 NBA draft, being selected by the Golden State Warriors. But Murphy barely attempted any 3s in his first 3 years in the league. Over his first 3 years in the NBA, Murphy ATTEMPTED a combined total of 40 3's. Though we know Murphy worked extremely hard during the 2004 offseason (after his 3rd NBA season), some moves must have been made that summer by the Warriors front office, which certainly complimented Murphy better. That next season, Troy Murphy attempted 148 3-pointers and averaged 15.4 points per game. But he'd only be on the Warriors for two seasons before being traded to the Pacers. He wasn't horrible in Indiana, he averaged double-digit points and rebounds while starting at center. But after 4 seasons in Indiana, Murphy was traded to the New Jersey Nets, where his career went downhill.

Murphy had an average NBA career, as he was a solid scorer and a good starter for 7 NBA seasons. But did he reach his full potential? Not at all. He could have been a consistent all-star, and with his scoring, maybe more.

But what did Troy Murphy have around him, which made him the player he was? What changes did the Warriors make in the 2004 offseason which turned him from a fringe starter to an NBA's most improved player candidate? Why did he average more rebounds on the Pacers, but shot more 3's on the Warriors? Well, to dig deeper, let's look at what a "stretch 4" needs around him to be the most effective.

Belief is the most important part, especially for a shooting big. The shooting big's coach and GM have to believe in him and his shooting abilities enough to put the ball in his hand for a majority of the team's offensive possessions. Not only does the shooting big have to be his team's #1 scoring option, he also needs the ball outside the paint and around the perimeter. This would be going against the norm, so the coach and GM would have to really believe in the shooting big.

Secondly, the shooting big needs a pass-first point guard. This point guard has to be an exceptional playmaker and has to always be on the lookout for the shooting big. Open shots are extremely precious for a coveted shooter, so having a playmaker that can find the shooter when open is very valuable. But having a great playmaker with a strong basketball IQ is even more valuable for a shooting big. While most shooters who are guards and forwards can create their own shot, shooting bigs lack speed and ball-handling abilities to create their own shot. Thus, having a good playmaker would allow them to take more good and open shots, and less contested ones.

Lastly, a scoring forward needs to be paired in the front court with two inside scorers, an inside scoring big and a slasher. This would be a big help for the shooting big. With two scoring threats inside the paint, there will be many defenders clogging that area of the court. Likely, the defender guarding the shooting big will help on one of the inside scoring threats, as teams would rather give up an outside shot than an inside one. Strong defense inside means lack of defense on the perimeter: which is what shooters love to hear. They will get tons of easy scoring opportunities.

Some of the best scoring bigs in NBA history have thrived with these pieces around them. Let's start with Dirk Nowitzki, one of the greatest players in his era, is arguably the greatest stretch 4 in NBA history. Standing at 7 feet tall, Nowitzki was an amazing shooter. Like Murphy, Nowitzki wasn't very athletic but made up for it with his basketball IQ.

But Dirk was very fortunate and lucky to have what he had around him. He had the most important thing: belief. Don Nelson, the Mavericks coach at the time, strongly believed in him. He traded for Nowitzki in the 1998 NBA draft, believing he could be one of the best shooting bigs to ever play the game. Though Nowitzki had a poor first season, Nelson continued to believe in Nowitzki. In 1999, Mark Cuban bought the Mavericks. Cuban was another strong believer in Dirk, and worked his hardest to surround Dirk with the necessary talent to succeed.

Nowitzki ALWAYS played with a great playmaker. In his prime, from 1998-2004, Dirk played alongside Steve Nash, one of the greatest passers in NBA history. At this point,

Nash has yet to hit his peak, as he'd leave the Mavericks for the Phoenix Suns in 2004 and win 2 MVP's there, but he was still an exceptional passer. Nash played 6 seasons in Dallas and averaged 7 or more assists per game.

The next 3 seasons, after Nash left, Dirk didn't play alongside any hall-of-fame point guard, but he was at the peak of his career. At that point in time, Dirk was at the pure top of his game and all he needed was a pass-first point guard to get him the ball and get out of the way. And he had that in Devin Harris, one of the best athletic playmakers of that time.

Dirk definitely would've declined after the 2008 season if he hadn't played alongside a great playmaker. His athleticism, which was already subpar, was declining at a rapid rate. Correlating with his declining athleticism was his declining ability to create shots, as he wasn't fast enough to consistently get past defenders and jump high enough to get his shot off mildly contested.

But he maintained the same all-star level of play for the next 5 years, until 2012 when he was 34. How? In 2008, the Mavericks traded for all-star point guard Jason Kidd. Kidd stands 2nd in all-time career assists, only behind John Stockton. He was definitely the best passer of the 2000's, and though he was past his prime, he still had his playmaking abilities. This had a huge effect on Dirk. In the 2009-2010 season, at the age of 32 and with limited athleticism, Dirk averaged 25 points per game and shot 42% from 3-point range. The next year, Dirk made 52% of his shots during the regular season and averaged 27 points per game in a playoff run where he led the Mavericks over the Lakers, Thunder, and Heat to clinch his first NBA championship.

It was in these seasons where the pieces around Dirk helped him the most. Despite having limited athleticism, he was still able to be one of the best players in the league. But it wasn't only Jason Kidd who helped elevate Dirk's play. He had the two other things which are very important for a stretch 4.

Belief, as I said earlier, is one of the most important things a stretch 4 can have. And Dirk has had it all the way through. Even now, at the age of 39, the Mavericks are still trying to build their team around him. The loyalty the Mavericks organization is showing Dirk is simply insane. And it all comes from one man: Donnie Nelson. Donnie Nelson is the son of former Mavericks coach Don Nelson. As I mentioned earlier, Don Nelson was a strong believer in Nowitzki, and decided to complete a trade for him. Well, turns out Donnie Nelson may be an even stronger believer in Nowitzki.

Donnie took over the Mavericks front office in 2001, and still currently holds positions of general manager and president of basketball operations. Even now, when Dirk isn't even an all-star, Donnie is still giving Dirk all the tools to help Dirk play at a high level. He could have easily pulled Dirk to the bench and built a fast-paced, athletic team more suitable for today's style of play. But he hasn't. He has stayed loyal to Dirk, even at the cost of his team's success. This is one of the biggest reasons why Dirk has maintained such a high level of play.

Around him, Dirk not only had a hall-of-fame playmaker, he also had two great inside scorers. At the small forward, Dirk had Shawn Marion, one of the best slashers of that time. Marion had maintained an insanely high amount of athleticism, even into his 30s. He was a very poor jump shooter, but made up for it with his ability to get to the rim and convert on layups and dunks. At center, Dirk had Tyson Chandler, one of the most feared scoring centers of that time. Tyson had a high field goal percentage, and was a threat to score whenever he got the ball.

Did Troy have these pieces around him? Well, he had some pieces at some points in time. But he never had the most important thing: belief. He was never believed to be one of the best players in the league, never given the keys to lead a team. He was always regarded as a 3rd or 4th scoring option. Teams he played on took advantage of his size and rebounding ability more than his actual shooting abilities. When he was on the Pacers, Murphy was the starting center and mostly rebounded and took shots in the paint.

7

DOMINANT BIG

Dwight Howard was THE MAN when he played for the Orlando Magic. He was the most dominant center in the game and considered as one of the top 5 players in the league. He could do it all, both defensively and offensively.

Though the offensive numbers he put up were never spectacular (averaging no more than 23 points per game), the impact he had on the game was. Howard was possibly the most physical, dominant center to ever come around. Dwight was like Shaq, except much more athletic. Howard had much less body fat than Shaq, but was almost as strong. Though he wasn't was much of a presence in the post as Shaq (nobody will ever be), he made up for it with his jumping ability, as he was able to leap high and get almost every shot up in the post untouched.

Though Howard never actually put up any amazing scoring numbers, he still got the ball a lot in Orlando. For these dominant post players, once they start scoring, they get a lot of double teams and triple teams. While Shaq would still try to attempt shots over these double and triple teams, Howard instead tried to work the ball back to the perimeter for a good shot. This worked well for Howard and his team, as the Magic won a great amount when Howard was at his best (they made the finals).

However, Howard had some issues with the Orlando coaching staff and management. He requested a trade in the 2012 season, and ended up being traded to the Lakers in the 2012 summer.

Dwight to LA was one of the most heavily hyped trades in NBA history. Fans were very excited to see how Dwight Howard, Kobe Bryant, Pau Gasol, and (the recently acquired) Steve Nash would all work together. Many expected the Lakers to win 60+ games that year.

But the Lakers ended up going below expectations and only winning 45 games, which barely got them to the play-offs. One large reason for this was the production of Dwight Howard. Though his numbers didn't drop significantly, his production and efficiency definitely did. While Dwight was easily putting up 23 points per game in Orlando, in LA he struggled to put up 17. His field goal percentage dropped by 5%. Dwight wasn't the man anymore, he was turning into just another center. He wasn't making significant impacts on the floor. He wasn't himself.

And this has been the Dwight we've seen for the past 5 years. Though Dwight has changed teams numerous times, his production and impact on the game has never been close to what it was in Orlando.

Why did Howard decline like this? How did he go from the best big man in the NBA to an average center? Maybe because it was the players he played with in Orlando versus the players he played with in Los Angeles. While it takes many good seasons to build up an athlete's confidence, it might take just one bad season to break it. A bad season in

LA probably wrecked Dwight's confidence, especially considered with the expectations he was set up with and the criticism he was faced for not living up to them.

To compare Dwight's teammates in Orlando versus them in Los Angeles, we first have to see what a dominant big man needs around him to succeed. First of all, a dominant big man needs the ball, a lot. A dominant big man can't be effective unless he is the center of a team's offense. He may not be shooting every possession, but he definitely needs to touch the ball every possession. Sometimes, he'd back down and get a shot up. Other times, he'd back down and pass out of a double team, or find someone open from the post. These types of players rarely force shots, which is the reason for their high field goal percentages. It takes time for dominant bigs to score. Thus, it's important that the dominant big is the focal point of his team's offense.

But a big man can't win games by himself, he needs other scorers. And pairing a dominant big with a slasher is almost the perfect combination. A team with a dominant big would typically center around dumping the ball down low for the big to go to work in the post. But once the big converts 2 to 3 times, the defense would start double or triple teaming him. Once this happens, the ideal thing for the big to do is to pass the ball outside to the perimeter.

A couple of swings would get the ball in the hands of the slasher. The defense, at this time, won't be in a position to stop the drive. Naturally, a defender would rush to close out on the player with the ball (in this case the slasher). The defender won't be on balance, however. A pump fake would cause the defender to jump and would allow the slasher to drive past him. Once the slasher beats this defender, he basically has nobody else to beat.

With a lane to the basket wide open, the defense would

likely try to rotate to prevent a layup. But most good slashers could still get a good inside shot up, even when the defense is rotating to stop them. This would send a message to the defense to also stop the slasher. They would get into a defense which would somewhat try to prevent the drive, thus easing a bit off the dominant big.

With the slasher attracting more defense, the dominant big would start getting the ball again. And it would only be a matter of time before the defense brings the double teams back to the dominant big. But the defense would also somewhat pay attention to the slasher, not wanting to give up a drive to the basket. With the defense focusing solely on 2 guys (dominant big and slasher), the other 3 offensive players would have to step up. And with the big and slasher taking up the paint, these guys have to be able to bury shots from the perimeter. This is why it is very important to have 3 jump-shooters complementing the big man and slasher.

Yes, I said 3, with two guards as well as the 4 (power forward). Having the power forward as a stretch 4 is very important because it keeps the paint solely for the dominant big and slasher at times. When the double team comes, the dominant big can just kick the ball out to one of the shooters. With the defense focusing on the big/slasher, these shooters will likely be left unguarded. All it takes is one made shot for a shooter to get going. Once the perimeter shooters get hot, the defense would have to alter their strategy and pay more attention to the shooter. This comes back full circle, as the defense would be watching the drive and preparing to close out on the jump shot.

Shaquille O'Neal is arguably the most dominant player in NBA history, whether he was playing for the Magic or the Lakers. Let's start off with Shaq on the Orlando Magic.

In Orlando, Shaq had Penny Hardaway, one of the best

slashers in the 90's. Penny was so good that he drew compar-
isons to Michael Jordan. Standing at 6'7, Penny was incred-
ibly athletic, with great speed and a high vertical leap.
Penny and Shaq were also complimented by many great
shooters. Nick Anderson and Dennis Scott were two of the
best shooters of the 90's. Dennis Scott led the NBA in 3's
made in 1996, with 267. This was the record for 3 pointers
made in a season, until Stephen Curry broke it in 2013.
Horace Grant was the starting forward for the Magic, and he
was somewhat a stretch 4, as he took most of his shots from
midrange and the perimeter.

In Los Angeles, Shaq was paired up with Kobe Bryant,
one of the greatest players in NBA history. In his prime,
Kobe was purely a slasher. Like Penny, Kobe was 6'7. But
Kobe was even more athletic, and he was simply a killer. He
was chasing Jordan, and he is probably the closest player to
Jordan. Kobe was smart, however, and bought into the
system of dumping the ball into Shaq, so the Lakers could
win 3 championships in a row. But Kobe was one of those
players, even in his prime that you could put 3 guys on, but
still, couldn't stop. He could score 50 points on any given
night and attracted a lot of the defense away from Shaq
(which is one of the reasons why the two were so good).
Shaq and Kobe were so good that they probably could have
won some games alone. But to win 3 straight championships
and to reach 4 finals in 5 years, Kobe and Shaq also had
some clutch shooters. Derek Fisher, Rick Fox, and Robert
Horry. These guys knocked down some of the biggest shots
in Lakers history. Whenever the paint was clogged up, the
ball was just thrown out to one of the shooters, who would
convert most of the time.

Howard did have these pieces around him while on the
Magic. At his best (offensively) Howard was playing with

Vince Carter, arguably the greatest dunker of all time. Now this version of Vince Carter may not have been the most athletic one, but he could still score with pure ease. He was still a big scoring threat, and he still attracted defense. Along with Vince and Dwight were some spectacular shooters in Ryan Anderson, JJ Redick, and Rashard Lewis.

Did Dwight have these pieces with him in LA? Nope, not at all. Kobe was old and had become an isolation specialist. The Lakers didn't really have any players, and Pau Gasol was another player who played in the paint. But the worst part was that Dwight rarely got the ball in LA. Kobe took most of the shots, and Dwight had to force many shots in order to even get 17 points per game.

8

WRAP UP

I n this book, we've looked at the big impact that surrounding factors have on NBA players. We've seen some players that had the potential to be superstars, but were average players because their surrounding players didn't fit them. We've seen others who've lucked out and reached their full potential BECAUSE they were on a team with players whose skillsets fit theirs perfectly.

Without realizing it, great teams have definitely used the principles of surrounding factors. They have built their teams in a way that caters to players fitting with each other. Teams like the Pistons and Warriors have built championship teams with only draft picks and minor acquisitions, but in a smart way utilizing the principles of surrounding factors. Let's see how they've done it.

Let's first look at the Detroit Pistons. From 1995 till 2000, the Pistons were led by a player named Grant Hill. Hill was a kind of like a LeBron James before LeBron James. He was athletically gifted and could score at will whenever he wanted to, however also had great playmaking and rebounding abilities. He was arguably one of the best all-around players in the NBA during the latter half of the 1990s.

However, after the 2000 NBA playoffs, Grant Hill decided to leave the Pistons and team up with Tracy McGrady in Orlando. Without Hill, the Pistons were in complete rebuilding mode. However, Pistons President of Basketball Operations, Joe Dumars, knew a good place to start. He negotiated a sign-and-trade with the Orlando Magic, meaning that (the Magic) would have to give away one of their players in return for Grant Hill. This sign-and-trade deal was beneficial for both teams. Detroit was desperate to get anybody back in the deal to rebuild around, while Orlando wanted to clear up cap space to give Grant Hill a long-term contract, and still have cap room to pursue Tracy McGrady and Tim Duncan.

In the sign-and-trade deal, the Pistons got Ben Wallace and Chucky Atkins. Though Atkins was only a reliable backup point guard for the Pistons, Wallace proved to be someone that the Pistons could build around. Ben Wallace was a hard-nosed, aggressive defensive center. Wallace was never too much of a scorer, however, he showed MAJOR flashes of potential on both blocking shots and rebounding. Wallace would come into his own on the Pistons, establishing himself as arguably the best defensive big man in the NBA. In the 2001-2002 season, his 2nd with the pistons, Wallace led the league in both rebounding (13.2 per game) and blocked shots (3.5 per game). Detroit was solid on the defensive end, which got even better in the 2002 NBA draft. In that year's draft, the Pistons used a late first-round pick to select Tayshaun Prince, a strong perimeter defender from the University of Kentucky.

A stacked defensive team, Detroit lacked firepower on the offensive end. That would all change in the 2002 NBA offseason. Detroit would sign Chauncey Billups and trade for Richard Hamilton. Billups was a playmaking point guard who could also score the basketball. Richard Hamilton was a pure shooter and an exceptional scorer, averaging 20 points per game in his 3rd season before being traded to Detroit.

Looking at this team in the 2002-2003 NBA season, you'd think it was a championship contender built around Richard Hamilton. Hamilton was the leading scorer, and he was complimented with exactly what a perimeter scorer like himself needs: a playmaking point guard, an unselfish forward, and a defensive big.

However, though Richard Hamilton was the team's leading scorer, the Pistons were led by their point guard, Chauncey Billups. Billups was the one who had the ball the most, and the one who created shots for Hamilton, Tayshaun Prince, and Ben Wallace. Though the team was already indirectly built around Hamilton, it was one piece away from catering all of Billups needs as a playmaker. He already had shooters in Richard Hamilton and Tayshaun Prince. All he needed was an athletic scoring forward (Ben Wallace wasn't a very good scorer).

And Billups would get that forward in February of 2004, when the Pistons trade for NBA all-star Rasheed Wallace in a 3-team deal. Wallace could score the basketball, as he averaged 17 points per game with the Portland Trailblazers before he was traded to Detroit. Wallace was versatile as a scorer, as he could score inside the paint, as well as make jump shots. Wallace was also aggressive on the defensive end.

So, here is what Detroit's starting five looked like heading into the 2004 NBA playoffs: Chauncey Billups, Richard Hamilton, Tayshaun Prince, Rasheed Wallace, and

Ben Wallace. This team gelled perfectly, because you had a playmaker, shooters, inside scorers, a strong perimeter defender and spectacular interior defense.

This Piston team would end up beating the LA Lakers in the NBA finals. They would then make it to the Eastern Conference Finals every year for the next 4 years.

The Warriors also achieved success in the same way. After success with the "We Believe" team in 2007, the Warriors wouldn't make the playoffs in 2008 and 2009. However, they had the 7th pick in the 2009 NBA draft. With that pick, they selected Stephen Curry, a future franchise player.

Stephen Curry has always been an outside shooter. As I've stated in a previous chapter, there are four main things a shooting point guard needs on his team to be successful. He needs to be his team's number 1 scoring option, to be paired with a perimeter scorer and a point forward, and to play in a fast-paced offense.

In his first few years in the NBA, Steph did not have this. He was not the main option on the Warriors, as Monta Ellis (a shooting guard) was the team's leading scorer. Monta Ellis was a slasher, one who scored most of his points in isolation situations. As Monta was an iso player, the Warriors played a slow brand of basketball (as isolations take up much of the shot clock). The Warriors didn't have a point forward at the time, thus Steph Curry had to be the facilitator for the Warriors. Thus, he wasn't as effective as a scorer.

However, everything changed in 2012. The Warriors traded away Monta Ellis, now leaving Steph as the main scoring option for the Warriors. With Monta gone, the starting shooting guard position was given to Klay Thompson, the Warriors' 2011 1st round draft pick and an excellent perimeter shooter. In 2012, the Warriors drafted Draymond Green, who was, in fact, a power forward!

This left Steph as the #1 scoring option and with a point forward and another perimeter shooter. He picked up his game and became an all-star in 2013. But when the team hired Steve Kerr in 2014, the team quickly became one of the best in the NBA. This is because Steve Kerr ran a fast-paced offense, and in this system, Steph Curry thrived and became the NBA MVP.

This is the big picture of surrounding factors.

ABOUT THE AUTHOR

Pramukh (Proby) Shandilya is a freshman at Saratoga High School, Saratoga, California. He is an ardent fan of all-things basketball. So much so, that his friends in elementary school gave him the nickname "Proby" after none other than the basketball great, Kobe Bryant of the Los Angeles Lakers. The name has stuck since then!

Proby analyzes NBA seasons, predicts NBA trades and game outcomes. He shares these via videos and blogs on his website www.probysportz.com

Proby played basketball with the National Junior Basketball League in all divisions through his elementary and middle school years and won 3 championships. He's a big believer in giving back to the community, which he does by coaching younger kids in the Saratoga National Junior Basketball League. As head coach of a Division 3 team in the 2017-2018 season, Proby led the Saratoga Grizzlies to the league finals finishing as runners-up.

Connect with Proby

probyshan@gmail.com
www.linkedin.com/in/proby-shandilya

Made in the USA
San Bernardino, CA
16 June 2018